BY TRENT HARRIS

DREAM GARDEN PRESS
SALT LAKE CITY, UTAH 2006

Book design: Warren Archer
Book cover: Ed Bateman
Photograph of the author: Erick Ostling
Special thanks to Stefene Russell, David Wade, Melissa Sanders,
        Mike Sanders, and the Confusion Network Systems

Manufactured in the United States of America (including Utah)

Library of Congress Number: 96-070967
ISBN 10: 0942688-11-2
ISBN 13: 978-0-942688-11-5

First Edition
2 3 4 5

Dream Garden Press
268 South 200 East
Salt Lake City, Utah 84111

www.dreamgarden.com
books@dreamgarden.com

Contents

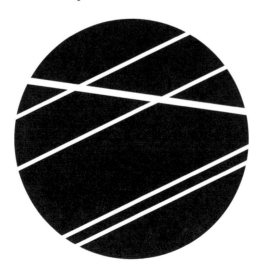

Multiply the number of seagulls at the Great Salt Lake by the number of crickets in Manti. Now take that sum and multiply it by the number of snobby bohemians at the Sundance Film Festival in Park City and you begin to appreciate the magnitude of the problem. Chronicling the bizarre in Utah is a project of biblical proportions. For decades, the beehive state has led the nation in peculiar stories about strange people doing weird things for unimaginable reasons.

Some of these people, like music mogul Melvin Dumar, stumble into the national consciousness for a week or two and then stumble right back out. Others, like mass murderer Ted Bundy, or mad bomber Mark Hoffmann, become infamous for their dastardly deeds. Then there are the Captain Nemos and the Cody Judys, folks that are just plain mixed up. Whether crazy, evil or dumb as a stick, these people all are serious contenders when it comes to grabbing national front page headlines.

Take these stories and scores of others, not as well known, lump all the strangeness together, and you have *Mondo Utah,* a state history the Centennial Committee would sooner forget.

It may be best to start with what mondo actually means. According to my brother, mondo is Italian for *world*. That may be true in Italy, but we are in Utah, a world unto itself. My use of the word comes from the 1960s cult film, *Mondo Cane*, which depicted world-wide weirdness and made the word "mondo" synonymous with "bizarre". It is impossible to squeeze all the bizarre events that have happened, and continue to happen in Utah, into one book. So I have selected just a few of my favorites. In this book I have also endeavored to give a more in-depth meaning of the word "mondo".

FIRST ENCOUNTERS OF THE WEIRD KIND

My first encounter with Mondo was at age nine. Uncle LeRoy and I were sitting in church, next to my grandmother. Uncle LeRoy had suffered a stroke and had not so much as mumbled a word in five years. Suddenly, in the middle of sacrament meeting, LeRoy stood up and shouted,

"Oh bullshit!" He then sat down, looked at the Bishop and said, "Go on with your speech, Gumby." It was at that moment that I developed what I call a benevolent respect for the bizarre.

GOD TELLS MAN TO DO DUMB THING

MONDO 1. A state of being in which one goes too far, not because one wants to, but because one must.

PAGE 5

S ometime in 1993, God told Cody Judy to tape batteries to an old radio and go to a BYU fireside meeting where apostle Howard H. Hunter of the Church of Jesus Christ of Latter-day Saints was speaking. Once there, Judy walked onto the stage, held his fake radio-bomb to the apostle's head, and announced that he, Cody Judy, was the new Prophet, Seer, and Revelator of the Mormon Church. 17,000 students sat silently for a moment, then spontaneously broke out in a rendition of "Thank Thee Oh God For Our Prophet." Judy thought they were sing to <u>him</u>. The tactic worked. Mr. Judy dropped his guard. Security jumped in and beat him to a pulp.

Mr. Judy was then put in a mental hospital for evaluation. While in the hospital, he had a dream that instructed him to "make like a vampire." This Judy did by hiding under his bed. While vampire Judy was under the bed, he devised a plan for escape. "I would definitely leave in the wee early hours of the hunter," he later wrote in a letter, and that he did. In the middle of the night,

Judy yanked the screen off a window and wormed his way to freedom. The police searched with bloodhounds and helicopters but vampire Judy was wise to the ways of the woods and managed to elude capture. He did this by going to the mountains and covering himself with leaves. He then, as he put it, "lived like a deer."

After three days, the leaf covered Prophet, Seer, and Revelator vampire grew tired of living like a deer and devised a new plan. He decided to become invisible. The invisible Mr. Judy then came down from the mountains and walked through Salt Lake City, undetected, to the lobby of KSL Channel 5. There he became visible and announced to the receptionist that he had arrived. She immediately alerted the authorities, and Mr. Judy was thrown back in the slammer.

This is Mondo.

ENID GREENE WALDHOLTZ IS NOT

MONDO

Congresswoman Enid did a tremendous job of grabbing the national spotlight in 1995 and 96, but she is not mondo. Yes, her husband Joe Waldholtz was accused of stealing all kinds of money from his grandma; and yes, Enid did fund a campaign about honesty and integrity using illegal money; and yes, she did admit to being a chucklehead for love while setting a world record for crying the longest on TV. And finally, I must admit there was a moment when the Enid saga nearly transcended to mondo status. It came right around the time the story broke about Enid's dog drinking only bottled water. Yes, it was when investigators discovered all those gay porn magazines in Enid's garage. Everyone suspected they were Joe's but...oh well.

In any case one must conclude that Enid is solely responsible for the mess she is in. *True Mondos have no choice. True Mondos are a force of nature.*

MONDO HALL OF FAME'R GYLL HUFF

For over a decade performer Gyll Huff has bewildered audiences throughout Utah. He doesn't sing, tell jokes, juggle or engage in any form of recognizable dramatic art. While there has been a great deal of speculation on what exactly it is Gyll Huff does do, no one can dispute that he is indeed famous...famous for nothing. He has been a great service to the community, as has his cat Thistle.

"TRYING TO RAPE A MAN IS LIKE TRYING TO STICK A MARSHMALLOW IN A PARKING METER"

Joyce McKinney

When you meet Joyce McKinney, you understand why hurricanes were named after women. The McKinney saga began in the mid 70's in Provo, at Frosty's Ice Cream Parlor. That's where Joyce, sitting in her Corvette, first laid eyes on Kirk Anderson, who was sitting in his Corvette. Kirk had a promising rock & roll band called Prodigy, and Joyce was working on her doctorate in drama at BYU. "I could hardly finish eating my pizza, I was that much in love," she later told me in an interview. According

to Joyce, things got a little hot and, even though she was "techni-cally still a virgin," she managed to get pregnant while she and Kirk were petting. "It was really weird," Joyce said, "because right after that was when Kirk disappeared." Technically still a virgin? I attempted to press Joyce further on this issue but got nowhere, so we moved on.

After Kirk's disappearance, Joyce moved to Los Angeles. There she worked as a motel maid, saved her pennies and hired a private detective to track down Kirk. The detective located Mr. Anderson in England, where he was serving an LDS mission. Joyce, now disillusioned with Mormonism, hopped a plane and flew to London. Here the story gets a little muddy, depending on whom you believe. Joyce claims she found Kirk and he got in her car willingly. Kirk said he was abducted at gun-point. All I can say for sure is that the press reported that when the police finally did get around to searching Joyce's luggage, they found a complete bridal trousseau, a toy replica of a Colt-38 pistol, and a bottle of ether mixed with chloroform.

In any case, Joyce took Kirk to the English countryside where she had rented a cottage and filled the refrigerator with Kirk's favorite soft drink. Once there, Joyce put on a sexy negligee, tied Kirk to the bed with some twine and ... *had her way with him*. It was Joyce's way of saying she loved him. When they got back to London, Kirk cried rape. It was his way of saying *the Devil made me do it*. Joyce was immediately thrown into jail. Joyce told me that the prosecutor at the trial later asked Kirk, "Were you unwilling on that first night that you made love to her?" "Well...," said Kirk, "I wasn't as unwilling the second and third time as I was the first."

England being what it is, Joyce instantly became a big celebrity and was let out on bail. She was invited to parties and movie premieres, and even got to dance three dances with one of the Bee Gees.

Things were looking pretty good for Joyce but then, as so often happens in these kind of cases, the other shoe dropped. Old pictures of McKinney on a motorcycle, wearing nothing but a pirate hat, started popping up. People began to suspect that perhaps McKinney had been more than just a motel maid in LA. Rumors about prostitution began to circulate. All through the trial Joyce had claimed simply to be a good girl trying to save her man from the evil clutches of the Mormon Church, but now these darned pirate pictures were putting a different spin on things. Feeling the heat Joyce came up with a plan. Using information she acquired at the Mormon Genealogy Bank in London she obtained a new identity. Disguised as a blind nun Joyce jumped bail and skipped the country.

Seven years later back in Salt Lake City, the inevitable happened. Joyce was arrested, once again, for following Kirk. She was charged with harassment and giving false identification to a police officer. Joyce was let out on bail and she immediately left the state.

It's been quite a while since I've heard from Miss McKinney and I must admit, in a scary kind of way, I miss her. Her last words still send chills of excitement down my spine. "I'm not so different, Trent", she purred. "There are a thousand Joyce McKinneys at BYU right now. Maybe five thousand."

Didn't Anyone in the Ward Notice Her Five-O'Clock Shadow?

I first became aware of the trials and tribulations of Bruce Jensen while standing in the Young Women's Values Garden, outside the Lion House in downtown Salt Lake City. Somehow I'd missed the story splattered all over the news, so my friend Scott filled me in. It goes something like this. It was at the University of Utah Medical Center, near the Coke machine, where Leasa, a surgeon in residence, met medical technician Bruce Jensen. One thing lead to another, and within a month Leasa told Bruce she was pregnant. The young couple was married, first in a civil ceremony, then later, sealed for all time and eternity in the Mormon Temple. Bruce and Leasa settled in Bountiful, where Leasa came down with a bad case of cancer and miscarried twins. After several years of marital bliss, Leasa turned up missing and the police were called in. The detectives acted quickly, and Leasa was soon found in Las Vegas, sporting a new mustache. Bruce was informed, "The good news is, we found your wife, and she never had cancer. The bad news is, she's a man." It turned out Leasa was really a Felix, Felix Urisote. And to make matters worse, Felix wasn't even a doctor. Bruce later conceded that sex with his wife had been "strange" but, as he said, "It was close enough to fool me." Now Bruce Jensen spends a lot of time in the mountains for therapeutic reasons because, according to Bruce, "The trees don't laugh."

PAGE 12

Sometime in 1862 Moroni Clawson was gunned down in the streets of Salt Lake City while trying to escape the law. Moroni had been arrested near Fish Springs for beating the shit out of then Utah Governor John Dawson. Dawson was a worm of a politician who had made unwanted advances upon a poor widow. The widow responded by beaning the Governor with a shovel. The Governor tried to keep the whole affair quiet which, of course, made the whole affair into a huge scandal.

Governor Dawson decided to take it on the lam so he hopped a stage and high tailed it out of town. Moroni and a bunch of his friends caught up to the Governor somewhere around Mountain Dell. If they just would have pummeled the Governor and gone home they probably would have been heroes, but they went and robbed the stage too.

Anyway when it came time to lay Moroni Clawson to rest a policeman named Henry Heath felt sorry for the destitute robber and bought Clawson a new set of clothes to be buried in. Clawson's brother, George, mad as heck about the whole thing, decided to move his brother's body closer to home. When they dug up Moroni's grave they found him naked as a berry. Madder than double heck now brother George demanded an explanation.

Perplexed, Heath and several other cops marched up to Third Avenue to the house of Jean Baptiste, the local gravedigger, to find out what they could. Baptiste's wife was feeble-minded and invited the police in. While she muttered they snooped. What the cops found were stacks of shoes and other items of clothing hoarded in boxes around the house. They approached Baptiste and he began sniveling and confessed he had indeed been stealing clothes from freshly buried bodies. This non-descript little twerp was in fact, a grave robbing ghoul.

To say the town was in an uproar would be a gross understatement. They threw Baptiste in jail where he sat while people tried to figure out something really terrible to do to him. After a few weeks they they came up with an idea. First they cut off Jean's ears and then they branded "Grave Robber" on his forehead. But the town was still mad so they slapped a ball and chain 'round his leg and banished him to Fremont Island in the middle of the Great Salt Lake.

Fremont Island is a deserted rock, inhospitable to all except the brine fly and the notorious no-see-ems. (For those that don't know, a no-see-em is a tiny flying gnat with the bite of a buzzsaw) No-see-ems actually love Fremont Island. In fact hundreds of billions of them vacation there every summer. I remember visiting Fremont Island once and thinking, "Boy, there's nothing quite like trying to catch your breath in a swarm of 100 billion no-see-ems." If you've never been in a swarm, let me tell you, they get into everything, your eyes, your mouth; Lucky for Baptiste he didn't have any ears. Ha! Ha! Ha!

Anyway, back to the story. The sheriffs responsible for dropping Baptiste off on the island swore Baptiste had never been shackled with ball and chain and they denied any kind of branding. They did however, say someone, they weren't quite sure who, had used indelible ink to write "Grave Robber" on Baptiste's head...whatever.

The question arises, if you don't put Baptiste in chains what's to keep him from bobbing right back to the mainland the next day? Every grade school kid in Utah knows it's impossible to sink in the lake because of all the salt. In any case the sheriffs said they didn't do it so okay.

Sometime later, upon visiting the island it was discovered that Baptiste was gone. The roof of the shack he lived in had been ripped off and there was a dead heifer nearby.

Thirty years later, duck hunters on the shore of the lake near the mouth of the Jordan River found a skeleton with a ball and chain clamped around its leg. I wonder who that was?

SPEEDEEOS

Imagine if you will, your nose squashed up around your eyebrows while your ears flap against the side of your skull like screen doors in a hurricane. Visualize geysers of drool spurting from your clenched jaw as all the blood in your body blasts out your butt. Now imagine yourself cackling like a frantic hyena as your brain turns to hot mush while you pee your pants blue. If you can picture all these things then you have a pretty good idea of what it's like to sit in the driver's seat of a rocket car going 600 mph across the salt flats. Speedeeos do it for fun.

JOHN COBB AND THE WORLD'S FASTEST AUTOMOBILE

I hope there's no one down there, ha ha" That's what the victim told her husband on July 17, 1983, just before entering an outhouse up Millcreek Canyon. She was preparing to do her duty when by chance she glanced into the hole beneath the wooden toilet seat and...surprise surprise, there was a face staring back.

From the first moment I heard this story I have tried to imagine what might have been going through the minds of both these individuals that first instant when their eyes met.

Did the guy, who turned out to be from Magna, try to come up with a plausible explanation of why he was standing down there, waste deep in shit, clutching a video camera? "Don't be alarmed ma'am. I'm just the Poop Inspector." And what went through her mind? "Oh, the Poop Inspector, well in that case everything's okay."

I've also tried to imagine, what kind of demon could possibly possess a man to lurk in the pit of an outhouse? Was he really a perv or just a confused Republican who'd heard it was a thrill to shoot crack and took it literally? Another puzzling aspect of this case: What exactly did the guy from Magna, whom for the purpose of this book I shall call "Stinky", hope to catch on video? Being an expert in filmmaking I can speak with some authority when I say there's not a lot of light at the bottom of an outhouse and, when somebody sits on top of you there's even less. That means the only thing Stinky could record would be the sounds. Let's try not to think about the sounds. We've all heard them and let's try not to think about them.

Another perplexing question; Do you suppose Stinky had a huge library of these tapes? Did he bring them out at swinging parties in Magna for a good laugh? "Hey everybody, listen to this one! Ha Ha Ha!"

Anyway, when the woman saw Stinky and his pottycam down amongst the used toilet paper she did the only sensible thing: She screamed.

This brought her husband running. He immediately assessed the situation and took action. He grabbed a big stick, went back in the outhouse, and began trying to poke Stinky.

This, according to Gene Lowin, the law enforcement officer with the forest service who was first on the scene, had little effect. However, according to Lowin, when the husband left the outhouse, perhaps to locate a bigger stick, the culprit escaped into the forest.

Now imagine what must be going through Stinky's mind. He's hiding behind a bush covered with shit watching policemen surround his truck. "I'll just walk down there and explain to them that I am in fact the Poop Inspector and this whole thing has been a terrible mistake. The police will understand. They're reasonable people."

According to officer Lowin, Stinky's terrible mistake was parking his truck right next to the outhouse. He was easily apprehended.

When I spoke with Lowin on the phone, years after this event, I detected a kind of sadness in the officer's voice. Lowin, who now lives in Monticello said, "It's just not as much fun up Millcreek anymore. Not since they put the toll booth at the mouth of the canyon. Millcreek used to be kinda famous. I remember finding all kinds of weird stuff, piles of panties, guys in high heels running through the trees. But no more. Now they charge an entry fee. That toll booth has really cut down on the wild life in the canyon."

Oh well, just another case of civilization encroaching on nature.

The Made for TV State

I can only speculate why so many movies-of-the-week are based on Utah events. There was the 'Executioner's Song,' about Gary Gilmore's trip to the firing squad. Then there was 'Stand-off At Marion.' That was about Adam Swapp, blowing up a church in order to resurrect his father-in-law, polygamist John Singer, who himself had been shot and killed by police for not sending his kids to public school.

There were actually two films about the Bradshaw Murders — that's the case where the socialite mother persuaded her not very smart son to kill her very rich father so she could make off with the money. Then there was that one about the guy who took over the Alta View Hospital with a gun because his wife had had her tubes tied. I think that was called 'Siege at Alta View.' So luckily a lot goes on here. "I guess we're just blessed."

Anonymous grip on a film crew shooting in Salt Lake City

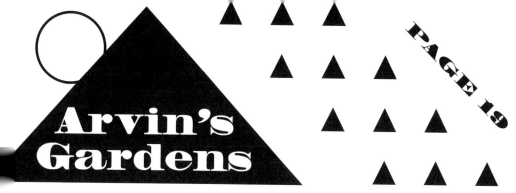

Arvin's Gardens

For reasons better left unsaid, many of our Utah Mondos are either polygamists or have some deep rooted fascination with under-clothing. Not long ago, in North Ogden, there was an interesting combination of these factors in the form of Arvin Shreeve and his Zion Society. Arvin, a soft-spoken, eloquent man, used his speaking skills in high school to become debate champion, and then to get himself elected student body president. He then went on an LDS mission, married in the Temple, and soon settled down as parks superintendent for Weber County, at which he excelled. Being a religious man, Arvin formed a church study group in his neighborhood. As head of the group, he began receiving revelations, not only for himself, but others as well. This got Arvin into trouble with his Bishop and Stake President, and eventually Arvin was excommunicated from the Mormon Church.

After Arvin's excommunication the Zion Society really started to catch on. A particularly popular part of the society was something called the "Sisters' Council." This was a group of about 25 women who shared in polygamous, not to mention lesbian, relationships ... and they liked to take pictures too. The Sisters' put out a pamphlet which stated their doctrine in the following way:

"*Begin to practice the Sexual Way of Life in all its aspects, especially the Art of Stimulation. Begin to apply, apply, and apply some more. Begin compiling an individual compilation with a description of yourself and photographs that the spirit confirms are representations of your sexual nature.*"

Another very popular part of The Sisters' Council was the lingerie shows. These private events were designed to sell the Sisters' own brand of lingerie which were painstakingly stitched together at one of the Society's ten houses. The nighties were called "Sweet Things". "Sweet Things", according to the Sisters' pamphlet, "help your dreams come true." To be sure, the lingerie came with catchy names and accessories. For instance, when you bought *Roped and Branded,* you got a free bandanna, rope and cuffs. *Wicked Witch* included a gown, drape and anklet. There was also *Pillow Talk, Dance Hall Girl, Pirate's Delight*, and my personal favorite, *Harem Dream.*

Arvin's Zion Society came crashing down when a private dick from Orem named Cheryl Naugle went undercover and joined the Sisters' Council. Cheryl's investigation revealed that the people in the group were cordial, overly sweet, glassy-eyed and kept very neat houses. Cheryl also exposed the fact that some of the lingerie models were girls under fourteen and, that when instructed, the girls would pull their nighties up in front of customers. Meanwhile, it seems Arvin was having sex with boys under the age of fourteen. He was convicted of sodomy and sent to prison.

MELVIN AND THE DREAMERS

A few years back, I drove to Layton, then headed west until I almost fell into the lake. There I found Melvin Dumar's house. When I arrived, Melvin had already assembled his band in his living room. They were rightly called "Melvin and the Dreamers". Melvin had just written a song to honor his wife, Bonnie Alisha. The song, called "Bonnie Alisha", went something like this. "Bonnie Alisha, Bonnie Alisha, Bonnie Alisha, Bonnie Alisha, Bonnie Alisha, Bonnie Alisha, Bonnie Alisha, Bonnie Alisha, I love you." The second verse was pretty much the same.

Most people remember Melvin as the guy from Willard, Utah who got himself into deep doo-doo by forging Howard Hughes' will. In that will, Hughes, the nutty recluse and multi-millionaire, named Melvin as the recipient of vast sums of money. At first, Melvin claimed he knew nothing about how the will ended up at the LDS Church office building in downtown Salt Lake City, but when his fingerprints were found smeared all over the thing Melvin felt compelled to change his story.

Melvin's new account of events went like this: Late one night, he picked up a disheveled hitchhiker in the middle of the Nevada desert. He sang a couple of his songs, and then deposited the tramp at a hotel in downtown Las Vegas. This tramp was none other than Howard Hughes himself.

Years later, after Hughe's death, men in suits delivered an envelope to Melvin at his gas station. According to Melvin, he peeked in the envelope, saw the will, got scared and decided to drop it at the Church office building in Salt Lake. Apparently Melvin hoped officials from the Church would have more credibility than a gas station attendant from Willard. Anyway, lawyers and the media tore into Melvin like pit bulls into pie, and he never got a dime, but Hollywood did make a movie about him, called "Melvin and Howard". It was right after the film hit the theaters that Melvin took time out from his new job selling frozen fish to start a music career. Last I heard Melvin hadn't made a dime off that, either.

All Dreamers Are Not Melvin

Ross LeBaron is one of the nicest people I've ever met. Not like his evil uncle Ervil. Ervil LeBaron was the leader of a vicious polygamist cult, The Church of the Lamb of God, that murdered many of its own members. Ross is nothing like that. Ross is gentle and funny, and he's also the greatest archaeologist in the world.

His discoveries include, but are not limited to, The Ark of the Covenant, The Holy Grail, King Arthur's tomb, and the tomb of Jesus Christ himself. He also knows exactly where Noah's Ark is. Most of Ross's discoveries are made within a few miles of his house near Kanab, Utah. The day I met Ross, we took a hike. After wandering through the desert for about an hour, we finally arrived and stood on what Ross called "very holy ground." We made our way up a hill past a few petroglyphs and into a cave. Ross announced that this was in fact the actual cave where Adam and Eve had lived. We then made our way into a smaller room in the cave where Ross announced that this was in fact Adam and Eve's master bedroom. I told Ross this was a fantastic discovery and that he should feel proud. Ross just smiled and said, "If I told you what I found yesterday, the world would catch on fire."

MONDO HALL OF FAME'R MIKE PECK

Mike Peck, the color blind house painter, joined the Mondo Hall of fame by creating a unique dialect of the English language in which every sentence begins with the phrase, "You fish lipped dog." He was also instrumental in the creation of the Buggolator, a device designed to electrocute brine flies at the marina.

I was lost in a blinding wind storm somewhere south of Moab when I came upon a sign announcing, "The Home of Truth". Since I have spent most of my life looking for such a place I decided to investigate. I ventured further out into the desert on the dirt road until I found another sign. This one informed me that I was too late. The Home of Truth was no more.

Imagine my surprise when years later I picked up a book called *Mormon Country*, by Wallace Stegner, opened it to page 331, and found out that Stegner too had run across the same signs. He however, had found some remnants of Truth and was able to answer many questions I had about the place.

Sometime in 1933 Marie Ogden packed up her belongings and her followers and left Boise, Idaho. The group traveled to the Utah desert where they created a compound known as *Marie Ogden's Home Of Truth Colony.*

The Home Of Truth was one of those Utopian places where everything was communal and semi-vegetarian. It consisted of the Outer, Middle, and Inner Portals. It was a place where Love-energy mixed with astral planes and spiritual forms. It was a place where everybody's actions were guided by Jesus. Actually it was mainly Marie Ogden's actions that were guided by Jesus and then Marie told everyone else what to do.

Marie Ogden picked that particular spot on the map to build her Home of Truth because it was at the axis of the earth. As far as I can determine the axis of the earth is a kind of west pole and, according to somebody's prophecy and somebody's revelation, that's the safest place to be when the end of the world hits. (variations on this idea are numerous and are in fact very popular in southern Utah)

Ogden bought the *San Juan Record,* the only newspaper in the county. In that paper Marie could print her ideas and revelations and nobody much minded. But then things changed.

What is it about religious cults, particularly ones in the desert? They always seem to start out with the best of intentions, only to end up

15 miles south of screwy. Unfortunately for Marie Ogden, her Home Of Truth suffered the same fate.

It was February 11, 1935 when one of Marie's followers, Edith Peshak, died. Marie insisted that Edith wasn't really dead at all. Marie knew this because her sixth sense detected "vibrations". Ogden claimed Edith was in some other worldly, astral planey, hooky-dooky kind of state, being purified, and would return to life soon. Marie then started distributing messages from the dead woman.

All this got the neighbors' attention, and rumors began to fly. There were tales of obscene ceremonies and early morning rituals, and things got really creepy.

Finally Sheriff Palmer ordered an investigation on sanitary grounds. The story made the papers in Salt Lake City and Edith Peshak's son, Frank, who was still living in Boise, heard about it. He hired a nurse and together they headed south to see what in the hell was going on.

Frank found his mommy was now a mummy, shrunken and blue-black. He screamed for her burial but, for reasons unclear, Edith remained up top of the ground waiting to wake up.

Two years went by. The weird rumors continued. Many of Marie Ogden's followers stopped following and left the Home of Truth. The place shut down to visitors and, just when things seemed to be quieting down, Marie came out with another declaration.

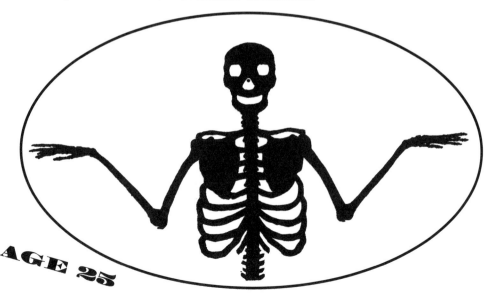

She announced to the world that Edith, whose new spiritual name was now Jessica-Edith, was vibrating like crazy and most certainly would come back to life sometime soon.

The authorities immediately revived the case and demanded a death certificate be signed for the Bureau of Vital Statistics. Marie said no, on the grounds that Jessica-Edith wasn't dead. The state said, Jessica-Edith is too dead. Marie Ogden said, t'is not. T'is too. T'is not. T'is too. T'is not.

About this time a character named Tommy Robertson popped up. He told a reporter that way back in 1935 he and Marie Ogden had wrapped old Edith up, dragged her down to a dry wash and put her on top of a big pile of wood. Then Tommy said he'd covered the mummy with a mattress soaked in oil and set the whole thing afire.

Marie Ogden had watched the cremation from a hill top. She instructed Tommy to gather up any of Edith's bones that were left and bury them right there on the hill where she stood.

Understandably Tommy wanted a souvenir of the event so he stuck a couple of Edith's vertebra in his pocket. Regrettably, according to Tommy, these two bones were later snitched and eaten by a sheep dog. Bummer.

Tommy Roberston's story pretty much let the cat out of the hot air bag when it came to Marie Ogden's Home Of Truth. The Utopian society went the way of the wind, as do so many dusty dreams in that part of the state.

PAGE 2

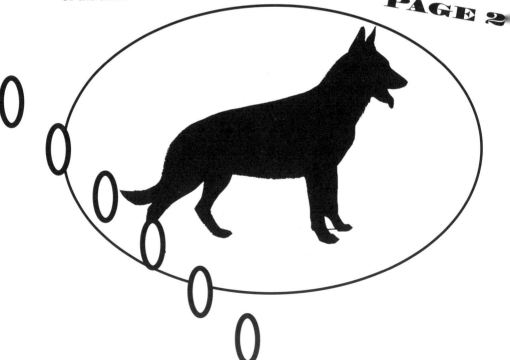

The Best Place Not To Pick Up Girls

Some things are so completely and utterly underwhelming that they deserve the designation Mondo. The Young Women Values Garden is such a place. The Garden is comprised of seven large flower pots with enameled signs protruding from the dirt, which sprout phrases such as "I am of infinite worth with my own divine mission which I will strive to fulfill," and "I will remain free by choosing good over evil and will accept responsibility for my choices." To really appreciate The Young Women Values Garden, you must understand that the LDS Church has located it in the courtyard outside the Lion House on South Temple. The Lion House is the barracks where Brigham Young, founder of Salt Lake City, Governor of the State of Deseret, and Second President of the Mormon Church, stabled twenty-seven of his wives. As an added twist, the State Historical Society has erected a plaque outside the Lion House that proclaims who built it and

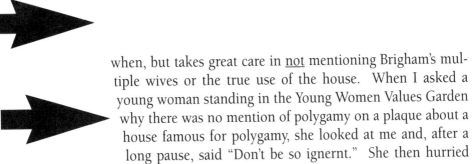

when, but takes great care in <u>not</u> mentioning Brigham's multiple wives or the true use of the house. When I asked a young woman standing in the Young Women Values Garden why there was no mention of polygamy on a plaque about a house famous for polygamy, she looked at me and, after a long pause, said "Don't be so ignernt." She then hurried away.

As if I were Mondo.

MR. BRICK PANTS

What it is that thing anyway?" Those are usually the first words to pop out when people visit Gilgal for the first time, and that's exactly what my first girl-friend, Jody, said on her first visit. "It's a Joseph Smith Sphinx," I whispered reverently. At that time I was in the 8th grade and still considered myself a Mormon. Jody stared at the huge granite sculpture for at least another 30 seconds and then said, "I know that, but what is it?" "It's a Joseph Smith Sphinx," I repeated even more reverently.

There are many mysteries in Utah, mysteries such as Jody herself, who at fourteen had the body of a Playboy centerfold. And then there's perhaps the most profound mystery of all, the mystery of the Joseph Smith Sphinx. Joseph Smith, founder and first Prophet, Seer and Revelator of the Mormon Church, had absolutely nothing to do with anything Egyptian, hence the fact that his face is sculpted onto a Sphinx the size of a Volkswagen has created a great many unanswerable questions, the biggest one being; why?

Created years ago by master stone mason Thomas B. Childs, the Sphinx, along with many of Child's other creations, rests in a garden known as Gilgal (a Biblical reference to a sacred place) which lies hidden behind the Chuck-A-Rama restaurant on 400 South in Salt Lake City. Gilgal can best be described as a vine-covered display of stone enigmas. Besides the Sphinx, there's a 3 foot long cricket made of rock, a large stone heart, and a granite sculpture of the giant in King Nebuchadnezar's dream. Boulder Head, nicknamed by locals because his head is actually a big boulder, is a 20-foot tall, sword-carrying statue guarding the west end of Gilgal. Featured prominently in the center of the garden is an impressive sculpture of Thomas B. Childs himself. The immortalized Childs, grasping blueprints in one hand and scriptures in the other, stands firm, sporting the only known pair of brick pants in the entire world.

Now, back to the mystery of the Joseph Smith Sphinx. It has been widely reported that the Sphinx is a symbolic representation of a statement made in the 1800s by Brigham Young, second Prophet, Seer and Revelator of the Mormon Church. Supposedly, Young declared that before the revela-

tions of Joseph Smith, priests in this world were, "as blind as Egyptian darkness." I say phooey to this theory. I know of no one that equates Egypt with darkness, and I see no connection between darkness, a sphinx, and the Chuck-A-Rama. And another thing, in trying to solve a mystery, it is important to ask yourself, what good is a mystery if it has been solved.

Jody ended up marrying a drunken bum from Sandy, but luckily the mystery of the sphinx lives on, at least until the property around Gilgal becomes so valuable that the descendants of Childs turn the place into the Chuck-A-View Condos; or worse still, King Nebuchadnezar's quick lube and miniature putt.

THE LEGEND OF EEENIE MEENIE

I have known many good dogs in my day, but only one that qualifies as Mondo. Eeenie Meenie is that dog. The only thing eeenie about Meeenie is his size. He looks like a rat with one ear. But to underestimate this dog is a great mistake. Eeenie Meenie has the courage of Rod Decker, the speed of a canary, and he's cunning...so cunning. My first encounter with Eeenie Meenie was in the summer of 1993. It was late, and I was opening the door to my place on the Avenues, when suddenly Eeenie sped out from behind a bush, bit me on the shin, ran in my house, ate a cube of butter, peed on the refrigerator, and disappeared into the night.

Others have seen Eeenie Meenie roaming the streets. Fools try to pet him. Bigger fools try to catch him. Eeenie Meenie will have none of it. He listens only to the wind.

My second encounter with Eeenie was several months later. I was sitting outside at Brumby's Bakery on 13th East. Suddenly, out of nowhere, Eeenie appeared. He attacked a Doberman and a Rotweiller

PAGE 32

that were tied to two different parking meters. Eeenie darted between the big dogs' legs, bit each one 15 times on the balls, and then ducked under a car out of reach. This drove the Doberman crazy. He broke his chain and attacked the Rotweiller. The Doberman's owner ran out of Brumby's and threw decaf latte on the dogs but they kept on fighting. Then the Rotweiller broke his chain and both beasts spun into the tables sending panicked people fleeing in all directions. That's when Eeenie darted out from beneath the car, his one ear flapping defiantly, his tiny tail, stiff as a nine inch nail, pointing straight at the heavens. He pawed the grass and snorted like a bull, then turned and, like Zorro, disappeared into the night. Yes, I love Eeenie Meenie. He is a rogue. He is his own master. He listens only to the wind...and if it blows the wrong way he bites the shit out of it.

OSCAR THE MUMMY

In 1975 Corky Nowell received a visit from advanced beings. He was sitting in his den when suddenly he was mysteriously transported to a place where the sky was bright and the lawn was like a golf green. He looked around and saw a big pyramid. "Why am I standing next to this huge pyramid?" he thought. Corky Nowell then saw a second building that looked like a flat ball so he went inside. Inside he saw really beautiful beings and immediately established a telepathic link. They guided him to a big crystal which Corky described as a modern urim and thummim. (seer stones used by the Prophet Joseph Smith to translate the Golden Plates into the Book Of Mormon).

On subsequent visits these beautiful people, called Summa Individuals, impressed still more concepts into the mind of Corky Nowell, concepts about the **Principles**. All this lead Corky Nowell to change his name to Amen Ra and to write a book called **SUMMUM**; *Sealed Except to the Open Mind*. This book discusses, among other things, **The Grand Principle**, which is the answer to the ultimate question of WHY and HOW the Creation exists.

Amen Ra, better known as "Corky" Ra, also felt compelled to build a pyramid, and so he did. The pyramid is in Salt Lake City at 707 West Genesee Avenue. This pyramid has become the meeting place for

Corky and like-minded people. Together they are known as the Summums.

Summums are an interesting bunch. They like to make wine and mummies. The wine is called Nectar and ranges in *suggested donations* from 10 bucks for a bottle of **Meditation**, to 50 bucks for a bottle of **Sexual Ecstasy**. The mummies are a different story.

The Summums have the only known patented mummification process in Utah. You can have yourself mummified, or your pet. Once you or your pet has passed into the other world the Summum's licensed and certified thanatogeneticists take over. First you're mummified, then put it in a Mummiform (sarcophagus). The mummiform is filled with Argon gas to kill bacteria then welded shut, and presto, Permanent Body Preservation. The process takes 60 to 90 days. Cats cost $4500. Custom mummies start at $14,000.

When Corky Ra's cat, Oscar, passed into the other world, Corky had him mummified. However, rather than put Oscar in a Mummiform, Corky Ra opted instead to have the his beloved pet gold leafed. Oscar now sits behind an altar in the pyramid, shining quietly over the wine-making Summums.

THE UNSOLVED MYSTERY OF THE WASATCH SNIFFER

A couple of years back, women from Ogden to Provo received packages in the mail. When they opened them, they discovered a pair of their own panties and a rambling, hand-written apology from the underwear thief. This in itself does not qualify as mondo. However, when you add the following facts a new picture emerges:

1. Some of the garments had been stolen years earlier.
2. Some of the women they belonged to had long since moved.
3. The panties still managed to find their way back to their rightful owners.

What we have now is a picture of a riddled with guilt panty-sniffer who really cares about his craft. He not only keeps meticulous records, but updates his records regularly. Perhaps he uses a computer or a color-coded card catalogue. "Let's see now, the pink Calvins from North Ogden which I liberated in August of 88, should be in drawer 3A next to the June of 85 lace g-strings from Orem." Whatever system he chooses, it is important to him to keep careful track of exactly where, from whom, and what he swiped.

That is mondo.

"I DON'T KNOW IF HE WAS REALLY WAITING FOR A BUS OR JUST WATCHING FEET."

There are men in this world who, at great risk to themselves and to others, are compelled to possess and *do as they will* with the foot apparel of strange women. Francisco Estrada Bonilla may be one of these men. He has been accused of attempting to steal shoes, not from a store, but right off the feet of female passers-by in Ogden.

Julie Berrett first encountered Mr. Bonilla when he stepped on the back of her heel in what she claims was an attempt to remove her shoe. It didn't work. She again encountered Bonilla the next day when he stepped on her foot again. This time the shoe came off. According to Berrett, Bonilla then pleaded for permission to put the shoe back on her foot. Berrett became suspicious and said no. Bonilla walked away mumbling. The third encounter came in an elevator where Mr. Bonilla allegedly eyed Berrett's sandals which were strapped to her feet in a such a fashion as to frustrate a person driven to steal shoes. "Those hard to get off?" Bonilla asked with evident depression. He then hurriedly exited the elevator and disappeared.

A few days later, Berrett spotted Bonilla again, this time while sitting on a bus bench. "I don't know if he was waiting for a bus or watching feet," Berrett later reported. Her suspicions growing, Berrett quickly alerted the authorities. "Later, I walked back to where the deputies had him surrounded and made the identification official," said Berrett. "He kept looking at me with such sad eyes. I told him I was sorry." Weber County declined to press charges, but transported Bonilla to Davis County where, yes, he was wanted for failing to appear in another case in which he allegedly knocked down a woman and ran off with her shoes.

(APTAIN MORONI

This action figure is a terrific gift for any child, or adult for that matter, who enjoys playing a good game of Book of Mormon.

WHY WOULD A MAN SODOMIZE A BIRD AT THE TRACY AVIARY?

ANSWER..Because he couldn't find a bird closer to home.
Or ... It was one hell of a good looking bird.
Or ... God told him to do it.

WILL EVERYONE IN OGDEN PLEASE CALM DOWN?

David Shane Shelby, sporting an orange jail jump-suit, stood and addressed the court. "For years, I've been listening to a voice in my head ... the commandments of God, and I obeyed them ... I was listening to God." I remember reading this statement in the paper and thinking to myself, God has a constant dialogue with the people in Utah. He guides our state legislators to pass incomprehensible liquor laws. He's in direct contact with every eight-year-old that gives a Sunday school talk. He even helps BYU win football games; so why is it so unreasonable to assume He'd devote a few minutes to talk to a fry cook at Arby's in Ogden? My question was answered when I read the next paragraph. It was there that Shelby explained that God had told him to build a light-bulb bomb and mail it to President Clinton. The bomb was intended to punish the President because he'd refused to follow Shelby's advice. Shelby wanted Clinton to fire Vice President Al Gore and replace him with Tex Watson. (Tex is the tall, dumb murderer whose only claim to fame is that he was Charles Manson's strongman.) I guess you could say Tex was Manson's Vice President, but I still don't think that qualifies him to be second in command of our country; and neither did the Judge. Shelby was sentenced to 24 years.

Never Laugh at a Lafferty

PAGE

There was an evil spirit roaming Judge Hansen's courtroom that day and his name was Moroni/Lucifer/Hitler. Ronald Watson Lafferty, facing a retrial for murder, watched as the evil spirit invaded the Judge's body. Acting accordingly, Lafferty jumped up and yelled "Fucking punk!" The Judge promptly ejected Lafferty from the proceedings.

Lafferty had once been a construction worker, a devout Mormon and a respected member of Highland, Utah's City Council. That was before he and his brothers formed a fundamentalist sect known as *The School Of The Prophets*. The School Of The Prophets, like so many religions in Utah, was obsessed with male authority, the end of the world, and divine revelation. In one particularly nasty revelation, God told Lafferty that he must "remove" his sister-in-law and her 15-month-old baby by slashing their throats. According to Lafferty, this act would clear the way for the Second Coming of Christ. After the murders, Lafferty was quickly captured and thrown into prison. It was there that Lafferty first met Moroni/Lucifer/Hitler, the evil homosexual spirit who, according to Lafferty, intends to invade his body by sneaking up his anus. (I'm not making this up, folks.) At times, to ward off Moroni/Lucifer/Hitler's advances, Lafferty attaches a piece of cloth to the seat of his pants. The cloth bears the words "Exit Only."

A uthor Frank Salisbury, one-time Director of the Plant Science Department at the State University of Utah, has compiled what could only be described as the world's most comprehensive collection of interviews about UFO sightings which occurred in the Unitah Basin near Vernal, Utah. This book, THE UTAH UFO DISPLAY: A BIOLOGIST'S REPORT, published by The Devin-Adair Company in 1974, contains the only known printed interview with Thyrena Daniels about the night she and her cat saw a UFO fly right over the top of the high school in Roosevelt. Other interviews include Tony Zufelt, who saw a UFO that looked like a box car with a flame

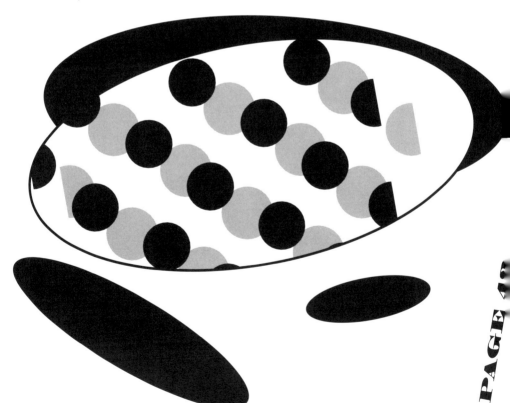

coming out its rear. Lee Albertson also spotted a particularly bright UFO while bow hunting near Buck Canyon. Albertson alleges that the UFO nearly, "scared the crap right out of me." He also points out that this UFO could not have been swamp gas because at the time of the sighting he was not in a swamp. Orvil and Czar Rudy were shocked when they made their sighting on the highway near Halfway Hollow. The UFO they spotted resembled a hay stack and traveled at a terrific speed. THE UTAH UFO DISPLAY: A BIOLOGIST'S REPORT contains several photographs of the actual highways where people actually stopped to look at UFOs. Featured prominently is a photograph of two model UFOs constructed by Junior Hicks and a graph explaining the ins and outs of the perplexing Mecham-Hullinger sighting. This book is a must for those still skeptical of Utah's alien roots.

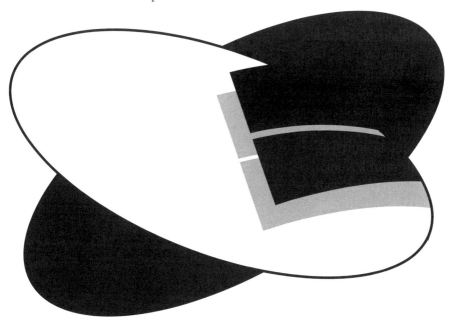

In 1944 a gang of sneaky pigs crept up on a farmer's truck parked in the Scipio Stockyard in central Utah. The swine then proceeded to eat the license plates off the truck and run away. That same year cows, dogs and deer also attacked and devoured defenseless Utah license plates.

It was the peak of World War II and metal shortages had many states making their license plates from materials other than metal. The Utah Tax Commission claimed their plates were made from pressed sawdust. However, a whistle blower named Tony Burdett, a one time officer of the Auto License Plate Collectors Association, claimed the plates were in fact made of pressed soybeans. Hence, hungry beasts wolfed them down like hot cakes.

Meter maids were mad because they couldn't issue citations and revenues from parking tickets plummeted. The Salt Lake Tribune referred to the plates as "flimsy, fragile, fugacious imitations...delusions and snares to both motorists and policemen." Finally the Tax Commission located enough

sheet metal to make 104,000 metal plates for the 1945 issue. The contract to make the plates went to the Gopher Stamp & Die Company...the Gopher Stamp & Die Company?

LUCKY SEVERSONGATE

his story goes back to my days as a television journalist working for KUTV in Salt Lake City. At that time I was preparing a report on a recent rash of cattle mutilations. Now, the easiest way to spot a cattle mutilation is to find a dead cow that has had its sex organs removed. Another clue is the surprising lack of blood or footprints around the dead animal. Theories abounded all over the place as to who the perpetrators of this crime might be. Some blamed UFOs, others said Devil worshippers were the culprits.

There was a report of a mutilated cow two miles north of Thiokol Plant 78 in Howell, and I went to investigate. Sheriff Redding had called Veterinarian Brent McKinnon to do an autopsy. Upon arriving, the doctor found the bull lying on his right side. The left ear, left eye, four inches of the penis, and the anal sphincter were missing. There were claw marks around the tail, head and along the back. It also appeared that the tongue had been chewed off. Upon internal examination it was

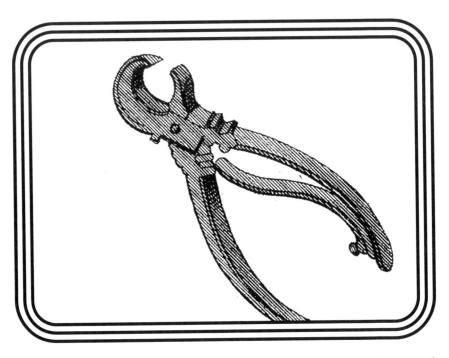

found that the animal died of a Massive Peritonitis caused by a nail puncture in the reticulum, or in other words, Traumatic Reticulo Peritonitis. The animal also had a Lumbar Pneumonia. The doctor determined that the animal had died of natural causes and mutilated after death by predators.

My deduction was somewhat different. I concluded that the bull had accidentally sat on a nail, and this had given the animal a heart attack. When the beast collapsed on the ground, a well trained team of cattle mutilators, probably government sponsored, rushed in, cut off the bull's dink and escaped in a black helicopter.

When I told Lucky Severson, Executive Producer of the show I was working for, that I needed more money to investigate exactly what the government intended to do with the bull's penis, I was immediately removed from the story. What was Severson trying to hide? How did they get to him? All I know for certain is that Lucky, who sometimes goes by the alias of John Severson, grew a beard, curled his hair and became a network correspondent in Tokyo, for which he receives a preposterously large salary for doing very little work at all. During that same period of time my journalistic career went straight into the toilet. I'll leave it to you to decide why.

LORD CECIL AND THE SEA OF ENERGY

Decades before University of Utah researchers Ponds and Fleischman began fiddling with cold fusion and the notion of limitless cheap energy, Dr. T. Henry Moray was busy obtaining a certificate as a poultry judge. Dr. Moray excelled at raising chickens, primarily Cornish Game Hens. He became somewhat of a legend in Utah, and was often referred to as the "Cornish King". One of Moray's finer birds, Lord Cecil, was crowed Grand Champion at the prestigious Sugarhouse bird show. Life was good and all seemed to be going well for the Cornish King until his wife received a mysterious phone call. A voice informed Mrs. Moray that her husband's life wasn't worth a plug nickel unless he learned to cooperate when it came to his other interest, the Radiant Energy Device.

Dr. Moray's Radiant Energy Device looked like a box. He claimed it trapped waves from outer space which originated in the fissionable reactions taking place in the stellar crucibles. According to Moray these waves constantly bathe the earth in a never-ending source of free energy and his box was a kind of outlet to plug us all in.

Dr. Moray wrote a book called The *Sea Of Energy In Which The Earth Floats* and then started demonstrating his gadget, the Radiant Energy Device, to folks all over the Salt Lake valley. When word got out about his invention he was contacted at his home on 2484 South Fifth East by Imperial Japan. Moray stated that the Japanese wanted him to use radiant energy to build them a death ray. He refused. The Russians wanted it too. They told Moray they would create the laboratory of his dreams if he would only come to the USSR. Again, he refused. Not long after that, a Soviet spy sneaked into his laboratory and smashed the

Radiant Energy Device with a hammer.

Dr. Moray bought a gun and installed bulletproof glass in his car. The glass saved his life when a black sedan took a shot at him and then sped away on 21st South. The culprits were most likely other scientists or thugs from Utah Power and Light, who wanted to silence him and keep him from revolutionizing the world with free energy. Then some mean sneaky bastard shot Moray's dog, King. Luckily, Moray and his nephew, Chester, were able to operate on King and save his life.

Yes, there are those that might say Dr. T. Henry Moray was paranoid. Well, I can say from experience that just because you're paranoid doesn't mean people aren't out to get you. I was shot at several times while writing this book, and someone named Bambi has been leaving pictures of totally naked girls on my car windshield.

Dr. Moray refused to let scientists, or anyone for that matter, look at the inner workings of his Radiant Energy Device so a lot of people thought the whole thing was just bunk. But dare I remind you that a lot of people thought cold fusion was just bunk too. Sure cold fusion fizzled out, but not before the Japanese bought it. And now, secret sources tell Mondo Utah that Sony has developed an inexpensive death ray which the company has dubbed The Lord Cecil Death Ray, and it will be available to consumers throughout Utah sometime before Christmas.

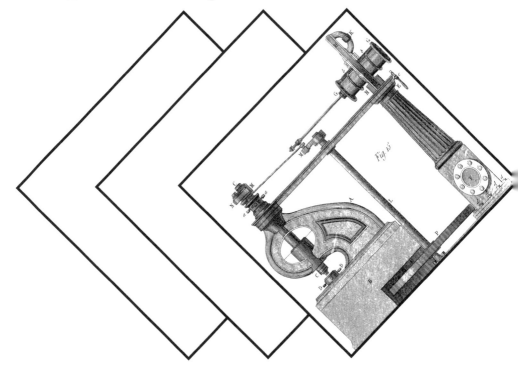

HEBER C. KIMBALL'S GRAND-DAUGHTER HAS SEX WITH NON-MORMONS!

Mormon patriarch Heber C. Kimball, one of the most powerful men in Utah in the late 1800s, had a great grand-daughter named Winifred Shaughnessy, better known as Wink. Some would say Wink *got around.* While attending school in Europe, young Wink became *romantically inclined* with a mad Russian dancer named Kosloff. So, like any girl in love, Wink changed her name to Natacha Rambova, joined the Imperial Russian Ballet, and went on tour with her new lover. Their rocky relationship lasted only until the jealous Kosloff pulled a gun and shot her. Wink survived her wounds and moved on to better things.

Still going by the name Natacha Rambova, Wink moved to Hollywood and designed costumes and sets for movies. That's where Heber's granddaughter met and married heart-throb-of-the-century, **Rudolph Valentino.** In fact, it was the girl with Utah roots that was instrumental in shaping the Latin lover's image, catapulting him to sex-god status. Rudolph died early, and once again Wink moved on to better things. She became a well-known playwright, an actress, a coutier and a spiritualist. She then went on to become a recognized scholar and Egyptologist who donated a huge collection of antiquities to the Utah Museum of Fine Art. Natacha Rambova is perhaps the best example of a smart, sexy, exciting and generous Mondo. I think I speak for most of Utah when I say, "thanks Wink".

THE ORIGINAL MR. MONDO HALL OF FAME'R

Brigham Young, was husband to over 50 wives, (only 27 officially recognized) founder of Salt Lake City, mastermind behind the Deseret Alphabet, (referred to elsewhere in this book) 2nd President of the LDS Church, Governor of Utah and pioneer extraordinaire. He was a man of remarkable vision and by far one of the most colorful figures in American history.

STEPS IN OVERCOMING MASTURBATION OR GET OUT OF THE BATHROOM FAST!

This handy pamphlet written by Mark E. Peterson, Council of the 12 Apostles, Church Of Jesus Christ Of Latter-Day-Saints, can be best described as the ultimate guide to self-control. The pamphlet assures us that by following the nine specific guidelines and the 21 suggestions anyone can be *cured* of this *difficulty*.

Since I didn't have the courage to ask the Church to let me reprint STEPS IN OVERCOMING MASTURBATION in MONDO UTAH I have done the next best thing. I have paraphrased it and underlined the best parts.

So, in the interest of public safety, here it is:

1. <u>*Never touch your private parts*</u>. Luckily, an exception to this rule applies when you are going to the bathroom.

PAGE 52

2. <u>*Force yourself to be with others.*</u> Make sure there is always someone else near enough to watch whatever you do.

3. <u>*Don't hang out with people that have this problem.*</u> There is nothing worse than a circle of jerks that can't control themselves. Break off their friendship.

4. <u>*Get out of the bathroom fast.*</u> Don't stand around admiring yourself in the mirror. Take short, cold showers and then quickly get into another room and sit with your mother or father.

5. <u>*Put several pairs of pajamas on.*</u> This will prevent any accidental fiddling while you sleep.

6. If you feel yourself being overcome by temptation, jump out of bed and go in the kitchen and <u>*fix yourself a snack.*</u> Remember, it is always better to eat than to fiddle.

7. <u>*Don't pray about your problem because this will only make you think of it.*</u> And if you are the kind of person that likes to thinks about *it* while praying, then you've got a really big problem not covered in this pamphlet.

Now if you've done all the above and your problem still persists, don't worry. You can also meet with your Priesthood Leader. He will help you develop a program to overcome your problem using the following suggestions. Remember, it is essential that a regular report is given to the Priesthood Leader so progress can be recognized and failures eliminated.

1. _Pray out loud_ when the temptation is at its worst.
2. Vigorous exercise; _double the amount when you feel your problem growing_.
3. When you feel really tempted to think nasty things, _yell STOP_ as loud as you can.
4. Make a pocket calendar, and every time you succumb to your problem _color that day black_. Keep up your calendar until you have at least three clear months or you run out of black ink.
5. Practice aversion therapy. For example, if you feel tempted to perform the act of fiddling, _picture yourself in a bathtub full of worms_ and then eat several of them as you _do the act_.
6. _A Book of Mormon firmly held in the hand_ in bed at night can be a big help in extreme cases.
7. In severe cases it may be necessary to _tie one hand to the bed frame_. (No, I'm not making this up either.)

Pause here and picture if you will... a young man wearing two pairs of pajama bottoms in a cold tub of worms, yelling "Stop!" as he prays out loud while fixing himself a snack with one hand tied to the faucet and the other grasping a Book of Mormon. Now imagine his family, watching from the other room, while he sadly marks another black spot on his calendar.

Why Us?

PAGE 55

Aperfectly reasonable question often asked in Utah is, "What the hell is going on here anyway?" We are a relatively small state in terms of population yet we have ten thousand more Mondos per capita than any place else on earth. Does it have something to do with the lake? Does magnetism play a part? Or, as so often has been speculated, is Utah in fact the center of a vortex? If we are at the center of a vortex then it is probably the mother of all vortexes. But, the question still remains, why did the vortex choose Utah as its home? After all a vortex can pop up any damn place it wants. Why is it rearing its ugly head right here in the middle of Zion?

Perhaps a more reasonable explanation of what is happening can be found by looking at the root cause. Perhaps the root cause is isolation, or temperature inversion, or inbreeding, or Mormonism, or radiation, or the desert, or mosquitoes. Perhaps there is no cause. Perhaps there is no reason. This would certainly be consistent with most of what happens here. But, unfortunately that still leaves the question, why us? Why here? What is it all about? Why can't I leave? Why do others come? Why does Jim Hansen get elected to Congress time and time again? It's maddening to think about. What if our Governor got up right now and said, Let us all join hands for a moment and not think. Would we do it? Would it make a difference?

Perhaps the answer lies where all answers lie. Right there between your big toe and your forehead. If that's the case then pick up your feet and kick yourself in the rear, and when push comes to shove, get out there and vote.

Subliminal Shoes

It was 1979 when Terry Jessop first alerted me to the fact that sex was sneaking into my mind. Jessop, who lived in the Provo area at the time, pointed at an ad for foot apparel in a magazine and stated, "Normally you do not find breasts on shoes." I stared at the picture for quite a while hoping to see the breasts, but had no luck. Jessop then showed me another ad, this time for Vodka. There was a picture of a liquor bottle resting on what seemed to me to be a table cloth next to two glasses filled with ice. He carefully studied the ad for a moment, then said, "It appears as if you are looking into the lap of a male nude person, and you can see...hair follicles."

Jessop had collected a whole book of these dirty ads to prove his theory that big time Madison Avenue advertising firms were subliminally using sexy words and images to subvert

our minds and make us buy their products. He'd begun a kind of one man crusade, lecturing to high schools, church groups and even the state Attorney General, hoping somehow to raise awareness of the problem and get it stopped. Jessop explained, "A moral person can shun these type of things when they see graffiti in a bathroom, but they are not prepared when it appears on Dole Pineapple Rings or angel food cake." Jessop then showed me an advertisement for cowboy boots in which a woman wearing cowboy boots was sitting on a log with her horse tied in the back ground. This one was a puzzler. Try as I may I couldn't see anything obscene in this ad. That was until Jessop pointed out that, "Women are not trained to sit in this type of a fashion. And also the use of a horse. Sex with horses is a really big thing on a national basis." It is? Maybe in Provo but surely not on a national basis.

Jessop pulled out one last ad. This one featured Sally Struthers, the actress from *All in The Family*. "Come on Terry." I said, "This is an ad for The Christian Children's Welfare Fund. You can't tell me they're wrapped up in this too?" Terry pointed out that Sally's right breast seemed much larger than normal. He called it the "The Dolly Parton effect." He then said if you squinted real hard it looked as if Sally wasn't wearing a blouse. Terry and I both squinted really hard at the ad and...he was right. Sally looked shirtless.

Wow, maybe Terry's on to something. He's obviously done more research than I ever will. And besides, I'm in debt. I need to sell a lot of these books. So, just to be safe, hidden within the pages of Mondo Utah are 17 breasts, 4 laps of male nude persons, and over a dozen subliminally hidden hair follicles. However, I have left out the horse just in case a kid accidentally gets a hold of this book.

KING RICHARD AND HIS YURT THAT NEVER WAS

"What's the use of reading books you already got? You can always get some more and read them, and then the ones you got you can read later." It's that kind of logic that makes Richard Daly stand out in a crowd. The truth is Richard read every damn book in his refrigerator. He also read every book in his oven, his bath tub, his cupboards and his closet. Richard had books piled from floor to ceiling. There wasn't one square inch of his apartment that wasn't covered by at least 37 books. He sat on books. He slept on books. He walked on books. He had books stacked outside his door because they wouldn't fit inside. There were birds building nests on books that sat on his window ledge. Are you getting the picture? Daly's room looked like a library after an earthquake, and Richard read every single word on every single page, and he remembered it all.

Richard's books were not your everyday kind of books. He read about the Sumarians, and the Babylonians, and dozens of other long-lost civilizations no one has ever heard of. He read about astrology and astronomy and water-skiing and King Arthur and airplanes and dogs and everything medieval. He liked stuff about genealogy and religion and archeology too.

All this stuff was rattling around in Richard's brain trying to get out, and when it did get out, it was truly something to behold. Richard would corner somebody and start waving his arms in the air, looking

like a balding orangutan. And then he'd start ranting. The subject was usually something like, how the Gates of Ishtar in Persia and the movie star, Ester Williams, were cosmically as inseparable as the Siamese twins born to the Queen of Iceland sometime right after the Great Bog Rebellion. Then he'd go on to explain that if you follow the lineage of that Queen and compare it to certain numbers in the Koran you will understand why Chevrolets are called Corvettes and not Siamese Bogsters, which in fact, would be more historically correct.

It was frightening. People thought he was a nut.

He worked washing dishes in retirement homes, saved every penny, and lived off the interest. He never bought clothes, or cars, or TVs or insurance or anything that normal people bought. The only purchase I ever remember Richard making was when he bought property up by Strawberry Reservoir. He would take the Greyhound to the middle of nowhere and make the bus driver let him off. Then Richard would walk a couple of miles to where his land was, look at it, read a book, and come home. He had plans to built a yurt (a tent kind of thing popular with Afgan nomads) on his land but never did. He was just too busy reading and doing dishes.

Richard started going to college and everyone that knew him got really nervous. Periodically all the stuff in Richard's brain would leap out at some poor unsuspecting professor and terrorize the bastard into tears.

We all took bets on when Richard would be thrown out of school but, I am happy to report, Richard outsmarted us all. Not only did he make it though school, but he was awarded a Ph.D. from the University of Utah in some subject having to do with connecting all the information in the universe into one big theory.

I really don't understand fundamentally what Richard's theory is, and I can tell you right now, there's no way in hell I'm going to ask.

Congratulations Richard.

OUR OWN DAMN ALPHABET

Brigham Young, in his 1852 address to the LDS April General Conference, said, "I have asked the Board Of Regents to cast out from their system of education the present orthography and written form of our language, that when my children are taught the graphic sign for A, it may always represent that individual sound only." What that means is that Brigham asked the guys at the newly formed University of Deseret to create a phonetic alphabet so that words could be spelled just like they sounded. And it came to pass that after great trials and tribulations the men on the hill did do that thing that Brigham had commanded, and that thing was called *The Deseret Alphabet,* published in 1869.

The Deseret Alphabet is an unbelievably confounding system comprised of 38 different symbols. Each symbol represents a different sound. An A (as in ate) looks like this Ɛ, and A (as is art) looks like this ƃ. The Deseret News printed a few cryptic articles in the Deseret Alphabet. Two school primers, the Book of Nephi, and the entire Book of Mormon were also printed, but basically the Deseret Alphabet died with Brigham Young.

So now, as the millennium approaches, it has come to pass that **Mondo Utah** has been given the calling to resurrect the Desert Alphabet, and to make it whole within the land, that many and all kindred tongues may wag in formation. In accordance with this calling we have provided an <u>official</u> *Mondo Utah Deseret Alphabet Decoder*, not to be confused with the *Plan 10 From Outer Space* <u>official</u> *Deseret Alphabet Decoder*. The Mondo decoder is more user-friendly. Now you can send secret messages to your friends, confound your enemies and have a heck of a good time at parties! We must also note that Deseret Alphabet computer fonts (IBM and MAC) can be obtained for 25 bucks by contacting Deseret Alphabet expert extraordinaire, Ed Bateman. His address is 2865 Brookburn Road, Salt Lake City, Utah 84109.

HE SEEN HIS UGLY SELF

Utah has a state bird, the seagull; a state flower, the Sego Lily; but as of the State Centennial, Utah still does not have a State Monster. After much research, I have come up with what I consider the two best candidates for State Monster.

First, the notorious Bear Lake Monster. This monster is apparently a mean monster because a report published in the Deseret News in the late 1800s has it chasing a family from Logan. The event was described in the following manner. "The creature was only frightened away by the family dog whose bark distracted it and caused it to look back at its ugly self as long as 25 box cars. He (the monster) then let loose with a flood of tears that washed him back into the lake."

Second candidate for State Monster is The Great Salt Lake Monster. This monster was first reported in 1877 by J.H. McNeil of Box Elder County. According to McNeil, he and several honest citizens saw the huge creature, with the body of a crocodile and the head of a horse, and heard its fearsome bellowing noises while it swam in the lake. McNeil reported that the monster so frightened he and his friends that they ran up a hill and hid in a bush. Further research on my part failed to reveal if this monster was mean. Since it is essential that a State Monster be both scary and mean, I hereby declare that the creature lurking beneath the waves of Bear Lake is the Official Utah State Monster. I also declare that from this moment on the beast shall be referred to in all legal documents as *Smokey the Bear Lake Monster*.

THE BUTCH CASSIDY MONSTER MOUNTAIN MUSEUM

"Since we live at the center of the universe here in Richfield, we figured it would be nice to have tourists stop by for more than just a hamburger." So says Paul Turner, former member of the Richfield City Council and creator of the Butch Cassidy Monster Mountain Museum. Ironically, Turner's Museum, a collection of over two hundred metal dinosaurs sculpted from tractor parts, car jacks, water heaters, and other material salvaged from the local dump, can no longer be found in Richfield. Turner's original vision was to transform a twenty-acre retention dam and collection pond on the outskirts of town into a park. There he planned on recreating several of the houses the notorious bandit Butch Cassidy once lived in. Turner hoped the houses, along with the dinosaur display, would grab the attention of passers-by traveling on Interstate 70.

Without experience in welding or sculpture, Turner, who runs a moving business in Richfield, began a four year labor of love to create his park. "I learned as I

went," says Turner. Using an air-cleaner for a body, and a horse comb for a head, Turner created a dinosaur called a *Cacops*. Old plow discs became the wings of an *Anurognathus*. Rusty sprockets and re-bar were twisted into the shape of a *Hypsognathus*. "They might not look exactly like the real dinosaurs, but the names and the dimensions are accurate" says Turner. His largest dinosaur is over fifty feet long, while others are the size of vise-grips. "My idea was to create every dinosaur that ever was, and, as more were discovered make them too." Turner finished about two hundred of his creatures before the Richfield City Council decided The Butch Cassidy Monster Mountain Museum wasn't exactly the tourist attraction they had in mind.

"Some of the folks said it was an eye-sore and we'll be known as a junk town if it stays up," says Turner. "If they couldn't catch the vision of what I was doing then it just wasn't worth the trouble, so I decided to take them off the mountain."

Turner had a few offers to purchase individual pieces, but he wasn't interested. "I want to keep them all together as a bunch," he said. So when Carl Hunt offered to put the entire collection around his Desert Inn Motel in Hanksville, Turner said okay. There are no replicas of Butch Cassidy's abodes and the nearest mountain is twenty miles away, but The Butch Cassidy Monster Mountain Museum is back in business.

"It works great for attracting people," says curator Hunt. "Especially foreign tourists. Germans go crazy for 'em." Admission to the museum is on the honor system. Visitors put their money in the wooden box near the *Tristychus* and walk right in.

MONDO THE MONUMENT

Yes, Congressman Jim Hansen loves Utah. He loves it so much he wants to sell chunks of it to Holland. Actually the chunks I'm speaking of are coal from southern Utah, and even though a Dutch company would make most the money off this deal, the black stuff itself would probably end up in Asia. There the coal would be burned and turned into smoke and power. The smoke would be used to make beautiful Utah-like sunsets and the power would be used to make things like souvenir rubber tomahawks that can then be shipped back to Utah and sold in Kanab. It's a hell of an idea when you think about it.

Hansen has always been on the forefront when it comes to "hell of and ideas" and therefore, I think its time we honored our Congressman with a monument of

his own. The President of the United States should immediately declare the west desert military test site as, *The Jim Hansen National Monumental Bombing Range and Antelope Preserve.* It's a park where the natural instincts of antelope to run go hand in hoof with man's need to bomb. This park would remain a sanctuary off limits to any and all environmental concerns, as would the surrounding study areas. These areas would include, but not be limited to; the ROWLEY CHEMICAL PLANT, famous for dumping more toxic pollutants into the air than any other plant in America, THE TOOELE NERVE GAS SUPPOSITORY, home to more strange bugs than you can shake a stick at, and the BING-HAM COPPER PIT, which is without a doubt the biggest man made hole in the entire world, unless you count that one in Argentina.

The Park could also be used to test some of Hansen's other ideas, like toll booths in the canyons and charging hikers money to take a walk.

And finally I think all of Utah should join together and thank Congressman Hansen by building him an asbestos lined, lead painted house. This house should be situated directly at the entrance to his park, right next to the Kennecott smelter and just west of the county landfill that he loves so much.

Big Balls Nemo

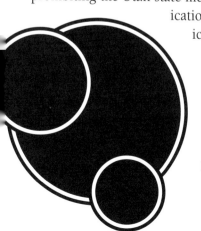

"I think they should test the doctors. One time they say I'm competent, and the next time they say I'm not." It would be enough to drive a guy nuts. And that's exactly why alleged murderer Eugene Woodland was complaining when he appeared at his competency hearing held in Salt Lake City. Woodland, who likes to dress up like Captain Nemo, the famous figure from the Jules Verne novel, *20000 Leagues Under The Sea*, and buzz around Utah lakes setting speed records in his fish finned speed boat christened *The Nautilus Missile,* sought and received a restraining order prohibiting the Utah state mental hospital from force feeding him medication and giving him what he called a "chemical lobotomy." At his competency hearing he stated that he was now okay. "I am right back to where I was 2 1/2 years ago." That's when, according to no fewer than six witnesses, Woodland put five slugs in contractor Bruce Larson who was busy transforming Woodland's repossessed *Captain Nemo's Dinner Club*

into a discotheque. Woodland steadfastly claimed he was the victim of a set-up. According to Woodland, he was on a routine walk when he was suddenly jumped and brutalized by two guys. Then rival real-estate developer Robert Massey somehow snuck the guns used to kill Larson and wound another man, into Nemo's pocket. "He (Massey) was the only one there who would have had anything to gain," Woodland stated.

Whether Woodland will ever get out of the State Mental Hospital and into prison is anyone's guess. However, anonymous sources close to the investigation revealed to this reporter that Woodland likes to be referred to as **Big Balls Nemo** when having sex.

Is This The Place?

A nude wise cracker at the This is the Place *monument*

ADMIRAL BEAVER'S BATTLE

John Perry Chaney, head of *The House of Chaney*, yet another off-shoot of the Mormon Church that believes girls are ready to wed as soon as they start menstruating, was charged with 2 second degree felonies for marrying off his 13-year-old daughter to his 48-year old friend Don Beaver. According to Chaney, his daughter was constantly trying to get Beaver into bed, and it was only a matter of time before Beaver would succumb. "If a 13-year-old girl wants sex, there is very little you can do to stop it." Therefore, to keep his daughter's honor intact, Chaney performed the ceremony which made his friend and his daughter Mr. and Mrs. Beaver. Chaney admits that at first, he didn't think it was such a good idea.

But then, as so often happens in these cases, he received a revelation from God. "Because Heavenly Father told me to give permission, I did." Prosecutors had a different take on the situation. They believed Chaney set the whole thing up so Mr. Beaver could have sex with Chaney's young daughter.

From his jail cell, Chaney tried to make his $200,000 bail by posting a $400,000 bogus check, called a comptroller warrant, signed by none other than LeRoy Switzer, head of the renegade Montana Freeman. If you remember, the Freeman were those guys in Montana who hated our government so much that they decided to create their own, even worse, government. The result was a marathon stand-off with the FBI that ended only when the FBI cut off the power to the Freeman's TV sets, forcing the Freeman to give up.

Anyway, when the court refused to accept Chaney's comptroller warrant check and give him $200,000 in change, Chaney threatened the judge with "prosecution for criminal conversion" and vowed to make the Judge pay 18 percent interest until the money was paid.

Chaney, wrapped in a jail blanket and wearing long underwear, also told the Judge that he only recognized the law of the Bible and common law and that he wasn't a person, as defined by statute, but only a sojourner on this planet. "Well, as long as you're sojourning you still need to abide by the law," Judge Burningham replied. That's when Chaney pulled a masterful legal maneuver. He filed a motion he called a "rectum rogare." In a nutshell, Chaney's "rectum rogare" stated that all Judges are biased because, at heart, they're really just attorneys. Back in his cell in Provo, Chaney continued his attack by deciding to go on a hunger strike. "I will not break my fast until I am out of here or dead." Then, concerned that the jailers might see his private parts, Chaney declared he would not take a shower until all the jail's surveillance cameras were turned off. The prisoners began to complain that Chaney was stinking up the jail and things started to get ugly. Chaney countered with, "There is no law or rule that says I have to take a shower." (I checked into this and Chaney is absolutely right. There is no law stating that John Perry Chaney must take a shower.)

At this point, I think it is important to understand that while all this was going on Chaney himself was married to a pregnant 15-year-old and ... the 15-year-old's mother is none other than Gloria Ward! (Thank you Jesus for this story.) Gloria Ward is that woman who holed up with the Montana Freeman in that afore mentioned stand off with the FBI.

After the FBI finally pried Gloria out of the Freeman compound, she ended up in court trying to keep custody of her two other unmarried daughters. The court alleged that Gloria had violated a 1995 court order by leaving Utah and moving in with the Freemans. Gloria insisted that was ridiculous, for she had merely been taking a vacation on the Freeman ranch when "circumstances" occurred. The Judge didn't buy it and gave custody of the daughters to

PAGE 71

the father, Robert Q. Gunn, long since divorced from Gloria Ward. Gloria then made a stunning declaration. She stated that Gunn wasn't really the father after all and therefore he couldn't rightfully take the children. The court reminded Gloria that 10 years earlier she had filed a paternity suit against Gunn claiming that he was indeed the father of her newly born child, and that she had demanded, and received, a DNA test to prove it.

Thinking quickly, Gloria countered again, stating that DNA tests were only 77% accurate. Still the judge refused to budge. Now it was Gloria's turn to pull a masterful legal maneuver. On June 25, 1995, acting as her own attorney, Gloria Ward evoked what she called "<u>The War Powers Act of 1933 and 1934</u>" under which she claimed a mother absolutely must be given custody of her children unless she is proven unfit. She then went on to show that she had no criminal record and no traffic tickets. The judge was still not impressed. Gloria pointed out to the Judge that he most certainly was subject to the "<u>War Powers Act of 1933, and 1934</u>" because his Court was an Admiralty Court, as shown by the fact that the US flag hanging in his court room was decorated with yellow fringe. Yellow fringe ...? Uhm ...?

At this point, I believe it important to clarify what it is Gloria might be talking about. In 1933 and 1934, Admirals were often seen wearing medals and ribbons and sometimes even fringe, and yes, yellow definitely is the color of a beaver's "rectum rogare." Therefore, and I want to make this perfectly clear, a comptroller warrant, as long as it is signed by LeRoy Switzer, can be redeemed upon demand at any post office for its weight in silver certificates or 3 cent stamps bearing the image of Demi Moore in a skunk suit. It's all in the Constitution. Now, if the judge is truly a prudent admiral, he will avoid 18% interest by giving Chaney his $200,000. He will then plug in the Freeman's TVs, and after a revelation, proclaim Gloria Ward to be the big bad Queen Of The House Of Chaney.

THE BIG QUESTION

While writing this book, several people have asked me, "Can I be a Mondo too?" I always answer: It's simple to be Mondo, but not easy. If you really want to be Mondo, you must always do the first thing that comes to your mind, no matter how dangerous, preposterous, or stupid. Do it with all your might and soul. Do it as if your life depended on it. Do it until you are arrested, and then claim you didn't really do it at all; or better still, claim God told you to do it. And if all that doesn't work, dress up like a clown.

PAGE 73

In July, 1996 a clown banged on the door of a mobile home in Ogden and demanded to see "Kathy". The baffled owner of the trailer stated to the clown that he did not know Kathy. At that point the clown became enraged, grabbed a $25 lamp from inside the trailer and began swinging it at the resident. After the scuffle, the angry clown fled.

Lt. Steve Turner of the Ogden Police Department was quoted by the A.P. as saying, "The girl the clown was looking for was the [clown's] girl-friend. This was apparently this guy's attempt to get back together with her."

Uhmmm?   Most men send flowers. Others shoot themselves or shoot their girl-friends. But as far as I know this is the first time a man has put on pur-ple hair, make-up and bedroom slippers, then attacked a stranger in a trailer park with a lamp in order to win back his sweetheart. I wonder if it worked? Did Kathy read the police report in the paper like I did and immediately call the clown? "Listen clown, I don't know why I left you for that rich tennis star with the PhD. I've always loved you and I always will...I love your lamp too." Or did she, like so many cold hearted women, shun the one man capable of truly deep feelings so she could live a pretend plastic life filled with riches where she thinks she is happy but really deep down inside she's just a mixed up little girl who will never know herself because she won't allow herself to really feel?

In Utah there's a good chance she went back to the clown.

Attack of the Giant Brine Shrimp

An unofficial poll taken in 1982 determined that more people in Salt Lake City had seen the film, ATTACK OF THE GIANT BRINE SHRIMP, than had read the Constitution of the United States. Completed in the early 70s, ATTACK OF THE GIANT BRINE SHRIMP instantly became a Utah cinematic legend, partly because there is something cathartic about watching a mutant crustacean wreak havoc upon your hometown, and partly because it spoke clearly to a fundamental truth so often ignored. I will speak to that truth later, but first a bit about the film's creator.

To say Mike Cassidy was obsessed would be like saying Madonna is vain. Obsessed just doesn't come close to defining the depth and breadth of his compulsion. Mike basically lived in his basement for 4 years creating his epic. I remember asking him, "What's it about Mike?" He said, "It's the saga of a naked pugilist prawn forced to grip a sexy violent town with its terrible tentacles of terror."...and there you have it.

Few people know that Mike had no splicer so he used Scotch Tape and a pin to stick his masterpiece together. His monster, the Brine Shrimp, was painstakingly constructed from a dozens of lobster tails gleaned late at night from the dumpsters of local fish markets. Using a slide projector and an old wind-up camera Mike created special effects more moving than anything Spielberg, with his billion dollar bud-

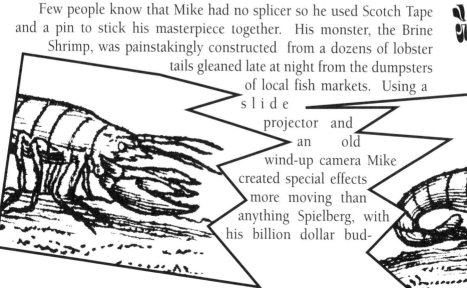

gets, will ever create.

To know ATTACK OF THE GIANT BRINE SHRIMP is to know Mike Cassidy. What Mike did was create a monster that would systematically destroy everything that Mike hated about Salt Lake. He hated the1960's Salt Palace. He said it looked like a hat box only not as interesting. Mike watched with glee as the Brine Shrimp ripped the roof off the complex. Mike hated Charlton Heston. He said Heston acted like a hat box only not as interesting. Mike howled when the Brine Shrimp smashed a theater marquee advertising *Omega Man*, one of Heston's worst movies. The monster then moved on to the Salt Lake Tribune where Mike had worked as a photographer. He hated the Trib. The shrimp tore the bejeesus right out of the place and Mike literally screamed with delight.

After a while Mike quit showing the film. He said that projectors scratched the print. I told him he'd spent 4 years making it and he ought to let people see it. He told me to shut up.

We took a trip once, our films under our arms, to explore the "scene" in California. We stayed with his aunt Florence in the Bay Area. One night we went to an open screening at the San Fransisco Art Institute that turned out not to be open at all. The guys running the thing showed a lot of angst-ridden experimental art films—you know, stationary shots of clocks ticking for 15 minutes, that kind of stuff. But when it came time to show ATTACK OF THE GIANT BRINE SHRIMP they

wouldn't do it. It wasn't art.

On we went to Hollywood. We were hungry filmmakers so we went to the *Bone Throne* on Hollywood Boulevard to get some ribs. The girl behind the counter thought Mike was Beau Bridges, the actor. Mike hated being mistaken for an actor. He threw a piece of "corn'licken chicken" at the girl and stormed out.

Then there was the time Mike went to New York and saw his hero, the great surrealist film director, Louis Bunel. Mike walked up to the maestro and said, "Hey, you're Louis Bunel and don't try and say you're not." Bunel stared at Mike with steely eyes and said, "I am not Louis Bunel. I am his twin brother, Louis." Mike went into hysterics. He cackled for ten days over this, repeating the story over and over. Finally, I told him I didn't think it was all that funny and he told me to shut up.

Perhaps the thing I liked best about Mike Cassidy was the fact that he loved to make films and he didn't give a shit about art. I think, in the end, that's why his film, ATTACK OF THE GIANT BRINE SHRIMP, will live forever, and all that stupid crap at the San Fransisco Art Institute will end up sucking the stinky ass of a cross-eyed grasshopper.

Mike Cassidy died of AIDS a few years back. Boy, I sure miss him.

MONDO HALL OF FAME'R ALEX CALDIERO

He is the flinger of flurious verbiage. He is Dada taken to its hair combing conclusion. He's new. He's improved. He is the cat who eats erasers.

Alex Caldiero's rise to Mondo can be attributed to his unique ability to put multiple objects in his mouth while performing poetry, and he does this while holding down a job in Orem.

Sister Bumgarden and the Tired Ox

"What is a Bumgarden anyway?" "Is it a garden filled with bums or is it a bum with flowers growing out of it?" "What does a bumgarden smell like?" "I really want to know!" My friend Mike Peck kept shouting out these questions as we entered the movie theater housed in the Joseph Smith Memorial Building in downtown Salt Lake City. We had come to watch "LEGACY", a film created by the Church Of Jesus Christ of Latter-day Saints to explain what the Mormons are all about to tourists. I had forced Mike to come with me in hopes he could add a few humorous observations about the film that would help me with my writing. As we entered the theater I was having second thoughts about that decision.

Sister Bumgarden who had politely greeted us at the door, now hid behind the curtains. She lowered the lights and the show began.

The bad news is "Legacy" has about as much to do with Mormon history as "The Adventures of Squanto" has to do with Native American culture. The good news is, that's what makes it MONDO.

One has to imagine that somewhere high up in the Church Office building a group of men sat around a table trying to figure out how best to present Mormonism to tourists. Apparently they came up with a plan:

1. Make a film that looks exactly like "Little House On the Prairie" only in 70 mm with Surround sound.
2. Leave out anything historically accurate.
3. Don't talk about what's actually in the "Book Of Mormon" and for God's sake, don't mention polygamy.

"Legacy's plot can best be summed up as, <u>Pretty pioneers overcome persistent persecution and tired oxen to found a town where the streets are straight and no one can bug them while they practice religious free-dom.</u> Now this is important because I have never met one single person who has said to me, "Trent, I really hate religious freedom." Except, that is, for my friend Mike, and he was drunk at the time. People may not actually like it when someone practices religious freedom, particularly if the someone is a Moonie or a Scientologist or a Branch Davidian who lives next door. But only a complete dope, (or Mike Peck) would go on record as being against religious freedom. Therein lies the strategy and genius of the LDS Church's well funded publicity machine. It works like this:

1. Never say anything a tourist can't happily agree with.
2. Never ever say anything Mike Peck would even remotely agree with.

If those two principals are followed religiously the Church will only grow.

"Legacy" opens in the olden days with Grandma Liza telling us about her first encounter with Joseph Smith, founder of the Mormon Church, and her eventual conversion to the religion. We then flash back to even older days and follow the young Liza, her Pa, her Ma, and her brother Johnny as they go through all kinds of pioneer-type problems. In one scene, Liza dumps her bald-headed boyfriend for a more handsome boyfriend and everything turns out fine. Intercut with Liza's romantic problems we see Mormons getting persecuted all over the place. One rationale the film gives for the Saints constantly being harassed by their neighbors is that Mormons don't like slavery. Score one for the Church here. Not one tourist in the screening I attended was for slavery, not even Mike Peck.

Anyway, Joseph Smith gets murdered about halfway through the movie. Mike started coughing at this point and had to leave the theater.

Things quieted down and the pioneers moved west. Liza and Pa were in real trouble now. One of the oxen pulling their covered wagon got tired and had to sit down in the middle of the prairie. Liza had a tearful talk with the beast about perseverance and by gosh, just as the music swelled, that ox got up and practically ran the rest of the way to Salt Lake. Now I've always liked stories about perseverance but I can tell you right now there is no way that could ever happen. This movie pretends a lot. It pretends that Joseph Smith looked like Tom Cruise and wasn't a polygamist, that blacks were welcome in the Church, and that the "Book Of Mormon" is simply a supplement to the Bible. It never mentions Danites, or Nephites or Zarahemla or white salamanders or the Urim and Thummim. There's nothing about the Jaradites in submarine type boats crossing the ocean in 600 BC, or Kolob, or the Doctrine of Eternal Progression, where men but not women get their own planet. And the filmmakers completely left out my favorite parts about Joseph Smith running for President of the United States, and Brigham Young wanting to start his own country, and the Mormon Wars, and the United Order. In short they ignored every damn fact about Mormonism that make it interesting. "Legacy" just pretends that pioneers were pretty and that oxen understand English.

There are however good things about this film. It is free. It is in focus. It does not star Eric Stoltz or Demi Moore, and in a fundamental way it says a lot about the Mormon Church. As my old writing teacher used to say, "What you choose to leave out can say as much as what you choose to put in." Perhaps Mike Peck summed it up best when after the closing credits he stood up and yelled, "Why not just tell it like it was, Man? You dudes know the real poop on the pioneers! What's your prob anyway?" Good question Mike. On the Calico to Crickets scale, this critic gives "Legacy" two chirps, five chirps constituting Celestial, zero chirps representing Outer Darkness.

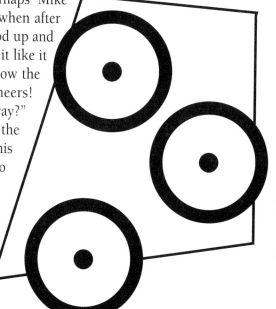

A FLOCK OF FLOPPING FOPS

Contrary to popular belief, actor Crispin Glover is not the only fop to grace our city of salt and charge an exorbitant ticket price to allow entrance to a show designed to educate and introduce bewildering aesthetic theories to an audience that really just came to look at a celebrity famous for acting weird.

Over a century before Crispin's *"Big Slide Show"* which he put on at the Tower Theater, there was an even bigger side show at the now defunct Salt Lake Theatre. The star of that 1882 event was none other than Oscar Wilde himself.

Wilde, best remembered as the author of **The Picture of Dorian Gray** and **The Importance of Being Earnest**, toured the U.S. for a while on the lecture circuit. There he gained the reputation as the Sunflower Apostle of the Aesthetic Movement.

One doesn't really need to be from London or Paris or Rome to appreciate the Aesthetic Movement but it helps. It was a movement in which the search for beauty was of paramount importance. To be a real practitioner of this movement it was important to surround your every day self with as much beauty as you could stand; beautiful paintings, beautiful dishes, beautiful door knobs, beautiful pets, etc., etc., etc....and it helped if you could write poetry too.

So, as you can imagine, when Wilde decided to come to Salt Lake City and enlighten the pioneers on the finer points of the Aesthetic Movement everybody got really excited.

Wilde arrived by train and, according to the Salt Lake Tribune, was the "observed of all observers." That's a polite way of saying people gawked. His reputation as a funny dresser who violated every

PAGE

rule of rhetoric had preceded him, so of course, young women waited near his hotel hoping for a brief encounter while young men, sporting sunflowers up their button holes, cruised the streets thirsting for even a glimpse of the famous personage.

Oscar was taken on a tour of Salt Lake City in which he saw the Tabernacle. He commented that it looked like an upside down soup kettle with furnishings suitable for a jail. He then went on to state that the people in Salt Lake City were very very ugly, particularly the women. And this coming from a guy that liked to wear knee britches.

Anyway, when Oscar finally made his appearance on stage he was sporting a lush black velvet coat, reams of ruffles, and black stockings, wisely selected to set off his stylish yet understated low pumps with silver buckles and pointy toes. He rambled for about 50 minutes about the virtues of the Lily and a bunch of other stuff. Some people clapped at the end and he left.

From all accounts Oscar's lecture was about as boring as a boot and had all the levity and wit of a bull moose's fart. But he did look funny and that counted for something.

Oscar told a reporter from the Deseret News "I am quite conscious that much of what I say may be annoying, but after all I came to say it, and so long as audiences with such forbearance and good breeding allow me to strut my brief hour upon the stage I should be singularly stupid not to take advantage of my hobbies." Who can argue with that?

Perhaps a more eloquent way of stating the same thing would be, as long as people want to dish out $15 bucks to Crispin so they can observe him while he shows slides he would have to be a complete dope to say no.

MRS. TIBBETS DROPS THE BIG ONE

The sun was blinding. It was 100 degrees but I felt cold. Goosebumps covered my arms. Chills ran up my spine. I was standing next to a dead dog, staring at an abandoned airplane hangar in Wendover, Utah.

It felt like no one had been there for years. The building's rusty tin roof flapped in the hot wind and made a sound like fingernails on a blackboard. A dust devil materialized and headed straight for me. I jumped into my car one second before the devil's whirling mass of dust hit.

I sat there, trapped in my car. My thoughts returned to the 60's, when I was in high school. Late one night I'd met an old man outside JB's Big Boy on State Street. The old man was crying. He told me he was the one that had dropped the A-bomb on Hiroshima and could he have a quarter. I emptied my pockets.

Two years later in Boston the same thing happened, different restaurant, different old man. I emptied my pockets again. Now I sat in my car with empty pockets staring at the hanger.

Over 50 years ago this air field had been home to the Air Force's

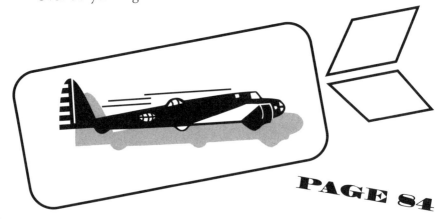

PAGE 84

509th Composite Group and this hangar had been home to the B29 that had dropped the A-bomb on Hiroshima.

I had two choices. I could get the hell outta there fast, or I could climb the fence. I climbed the fence.

The inside of the hangar was even weirder. The words *Enola Gay* were scribbled on one of the tin walls. Enola Gay was the name of Col. Paul Tibbets' mother. Col. Tibbets was the pilot in charge of dropping "Little Boy" (code name for the A-bomb) on the Japs. I wondered how his mother felt about the whole thing.

On the floor was an old Folger's coffee can next to a dead mouse. "Good to the last drop." For some reason the coffee can really gave me the willeys.

In 1995 the Smithsonian Museum prepared an exhibit in honor of the Enola Gay's 50th anniversary. A lot of people got mad. Some thought such things should not be honored, some people thought exactly the opposite. In any case, the Museum dumped their original idea for the exhibit and replaced it with a rinky-dink version designed not to offend. After all, the last thing anyone in the world wants is a controversy, particularly about the Atomic bomb.

I think the Smithsonian could have saved themselves a lot of time and money by designing a simpler exhibit, one that only included a rusty hangar, a dead dog, an old Folger's can, and budget allowing, a dust devil whirling up disturbing memories.

Keep 'em Flying

It was before sunrise in 1886 when John Koyle woke his wife and said, "Em - our cow that has been lost so long is down by the lower field with her right horn broken and crumpled so that it sticks in her eye. I dreamed it last night, and if the dream is true, that is all the testimony I need to believe the Gospel." Lo and behold, that morning Koyle found his lost cow and yes, the cow had somehow managed to stick herself in the eye with her own horn. Quick to recognize a miracle, Koyle immediately converted to Mormonism, went on a mission, and eventually became a Bishop.

It can be said that John Koyle had many unusual dreams in his life, but the most outstanding of them all came in the fall of 1894. Late that August night Koyle was visited by what he described as "a being from another world, dressed in white, and radiating intelligence." This radiating visitor led Koyle (in his spirit form) to a mountain near his home in Leland, Utah. Once there, Koyle and the visitor passed directly into the side of the hill. They traveled through the solid rock and eventually ended up in a series of caverns deep within the heart of the mountain. Koyle saw that these caverns were filled with gold and precious artifacts. He also noticed many records pertaining to a long-lost ancient civilization. Koyle described what he saw as "those Great Nephite treasures that are beyond your belief to imagine." (Nephites, according to the Book of Mormon, were an ancient tribe that once inhabited America).

After viewing the treasure the visitor instructed Koyle to dig shafts into the mountain and remove all the gold from within. Having no mining experience Koyle was somewhat reluctant, but after three more visits and a few more dreams, Koyle decided the visitor, whom he'd come to believe was in fact the Angel Moroni (the angel who was instrumental in starting the Mormon Church) meant business. So he complied.

Koyle formed a company and began selling stock, mainly to Mormons. His venture became known as "The Dream Mine".

All this caught the attention of the LDS Church's general authorities who were not happy with Koyle's mix of gold fever and religion. The authorities recommended that Church members steer clear of the whole venture. Prominent Mormon geologist, James Talmage, examined the site of the Dream Mine and pronounced that, dig as they may, they would never find gold in that spot. Others published articles discrediting Koyle and the mine. Still, people (some say as many as 9000) purchased stock.

At odds with the Church, Koyle was eventually released from his position as Bishop. He was reprimanded and even ridiculed but nothing could stop him from dreaming and digging, digging and dreaming, dreaming and digging. In the end he was excommunicated, the official reason given as "insubordination".

Years of hard labor produced nine mine shafts and miles of tunnels, but when Koyle finally died in 1949, he hadn't raised enough gold to fill his teeth. Koyle once told one of his nephews, "I can't understand why we haven't found gold. I did everything the Angel told me to do." Well John, that's what you get for listening to radiating beings. I mean, really. Next time hire a geologist.

In any case, cut to the 1980's: The mine has transferred hands and Ron and Dan Lafferty, the murderous polygamist brothers from Highland (referred to elsewhere in this book) are trying to get their paws on the property. They wanted to start something called the City of Refuge around the mine's base and use the Dream Mine as a rallying point to unite like-minded fundamentalists. Luckily for us all, that idea bombed.

Then came another polygamist, Bob Crossfield of Santaquin. Crossfield claimed he was in fact "the white-haired man from the north" that Koyle had prophesied about. Crossfield was speaking of a particular prophecy in which Koyle had revealed that

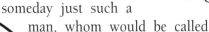

someday just such a man, whom would be called Echa Tah Echa Nah, would save the mine from terrible trouble. The mine was indeed in big trouble, Bob did in fact have white hair, and it can be argued that Santaquin is to the north. However, Crossfield's dream ended abruptly when after he revealed to the mine's new managers, who were good Mormons, that they would have to give up the Church when the mine started pumping out gold. Bob (Echa Tah Echa Nah) Crossfield was given the boot.

Accusations of fraud and embezzlement still center around what's left of the mine and its holdings. The IRS, and lots of other people, have a long list of questions as to where all the money raised ultimately went. Sadly, in the midst of the squabbles and scandals, the brilliant white ore processing mill built at the foot of the mine stands quiet, and no one ventures into the tunnels anymore to dig.

This brings me to an interesting point. Bishop Koyle made maps which detail the location of the nine caverns which hold the Nephite treasures. If you study these "dream maps", it is clear to see that the shafts he and his miners dug stop just yards from where Koyle swore pay dirt would be hit. Apparently the shaft's bottoms filled with water which made digging nearly impossible. Then, when Koyle died, people just kind of pooped out on the whole idea. So, now here we are, left with a mystery, an unfinished story, a scratch that can't be itched.

I propose a solution. Suppose we all chip in and rent some pumps, drain the water, and get the last 40 feet of the shaft dug. After all, why not find out what's down there? If it turns out to be nothing then we can all say, ha ha, Koyle was a kook. And, if instead we find "those Nephite Treasures that are beyond your belief to imagine", then I get the lion's share. It's only fair. After all, I heard it in a dream.

IF YOU'RE NOT PART OF THE MONDO, YOU'RE PART OF THE PROBLEM

Strange things do happen in this state, and they happen with great frequency. However pointless these events may appear on the surface, it is important to remember that they do serve a larger purpose. For as economic giants like Disney, K-Mart and MTV cram conformity down our collective throats, and powerful political forces, liberal and conservative, join together to rip any remnant of anarchy, lust, foolhardiness or fun from our souls, Mondos, and the lives they lead, continue to remind us that the world can never be tamed.

By their very nature Mondos are wild. They are different. They are dangerous. They stick their fingers in the fan so we don't have to. And, for all this we owe them a great deal.

Perhaps we should build a museum in downtown Salt Lake City, a kind of "Palace of Wonders" where all the Utah strangeness could be cataloged, studied and displayed. And around this great museum could be a special park filled with radiant energy and pyramids. And from this park the Governor could declare April 1 as, *Day of the Mondos*, an official state holiday. On that day each year we could have a parade, a big parade. Imagine thousands of Utah Mondos filling the streets, marching to the music of Melvin and the Dreamers. Joyce McKinney could be crowned "Mondo Queen" and wave from a float designed by the Wasatch Sniffer. The Sister's Council precision drill team could wear their carefully stitched nighties and pull them up in unison right in front of the Judge's stand. Then, just when you thought the parade was about to end, Eeenie Meanee, in a Zorro cape, could run out and bite Stinky from Magna right on the balls. If you are still thinking to yourself, "Well those Mondos are pretty darned entertaining but what good are they really?" then I leave you with this final thought.

For reasons unknown this state seems to nurture strangeness. Some might say it is Utah's way of protecting itself. They might say that this strangeness, is in fact, Utah's first line of defense against the rush to become California. For when Mr. and Mrs. Normal from Normal, Illinois, pick up their paper and read the latest news from the beehive state, and then they sit back and comfortably snicker, "Boy those dumb dorks in Utah sure are weird" and then they cancel there plans to move to Sandy, we can truly say we've won a battle, if not the war.

Rock on Mondos.

OFFICIAL MONDO UTAH DESERET DECODER

Deseret Alphabet Decoder

Long Sounds
e...as in eat...
a...as in ate...
ah...as in...art...
aw..as in...aught..
o...as in...oat...
oo...as in...ooze...

Short Sounds
as in...it...
as in...et...
as in...at...
as in...ot...
as in...ut...
as in..book...

"official"

Double Sounds
as in...ice...
as in...owl...
as in...woo...
as in...ye...
as in..h...

Consonants
p
b
t
d
ch..as in...cheese
g...as in..geo
k
ga..as in...gate
f
v
eth...as in thigh
the..as in..thy
s
z
esh..as in..flesh
zhe...as in vision
ur...as in...burn
l
m
n
eng..as in..length

Mondo Utah